Toothbrush People

American College Students' Personal
Experiences with Poverty, Inequalities,
Humility, and Kindness

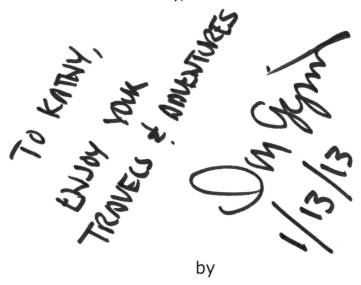

by

Don Gogniat and Valerie White

To Kevin,

Respect + Dyan Von Wagner

1/3/13
M. Shaw

Foreword

I have been very fortunate to have had the opportunity to travel and teach with the Semester at Sea program since 1985. Throughout my 6 voyages, I have had the pleasure of watching students "grow like bamboo" as they travel around the world. On three of these trips while teaching Global Studies I have given the same assignment to students in 1990, 2004, and 2010. This book is the direct result of that particular lecture on introspection. I sincerely appreciate the willingness of all students to be part of this work and share their experiences with you.

All proceeds from the sale of the book will be used for scholarships for future students in the program. It is nice to be able to give back to SAS; certainly the program has had a big impact on me.

Valerie White is a colleague and friend from my other life as an administrator at Penn State York. She has been able to provide an objective view of the importance and interest of this book for the general reading public. Her skills in terms of organization, editing, and publishing have been a tremendous help in finishing this project. All along the way she has helped to think through and guide the direction of the book. Although she has never been part of the Semester at Sea program (so far), her efforts certainly deserve co-authorship of this work. I truly appreciate her help and advice and hard work.

My wife has also put up with my travel bug and has been supportive through the years. With love, I co-dedicate my portion of this book to her. Dr. Robert N. Thomas encouraged me to graduate and become a geographer; I am always grateful.

And finally, as an administrator, I always ask faculty to consider building five educational components into their teaching plans. These are: critical thinking skills, group problem solving/team building techniques, ethical considerations, communication skills (verbal, written and technical), and a global perspective. Employers who are looking for potential leaders in their organization want to see all five of these skills/ values in the graduates they hire. This book unquestionably highlights the powerful impact of an international experience on students and how they gain a global perspective for their future life's work.

Don Gogniat

My senior year in college I travelled to what was then still the Soviet Union for a Jan Term course. Despite the cold, I was hooked on travel. My only regret was that I hadn't started going places earlier. Now my daughter, Emily, is a freshman in college and I am hopeful that she will incorporate study abroad into her education.

When Don asked for some assistance with this book, I was more than happy to help. As a librarian, I think anything book related has to be worthwhile. As a traveler, the Semester at Sea program sounds wonderful. The student reflections contained in this book exemplify how much personal growth can come from meeting people from different cultures. The photos and articles in this book are occasionally funny, often poignant, frequently sad, but all help to show how getting out in the world and making connections with others improves our own lives.

Valerie White

Why *Toothbrush People* is an Important Book for Students, Parents, Faculty, and College Administrators

As the entire title suggests, this book provides insight into American college students' experiences and reactions to poverty, inequality, humility, and kindness. Almost all of the stories (with the exception of one) are real life encounters students have had with strangers in other countries and cultures. In most cases, how they have internalized the interaction and why it is important to them is described in the narrative. How they have remembered the person and the interaction over time, is a compelling component of the second portion of the book, the 1990 and 2004 letters and stories.

While reading these stories, appreciate the relevance of an international educational experience as part of a college degree program. This book depicts only one memory from their adventures abroad. Undoubtedly there have been a multitude of such encounters throughout the semester. These experiences prepare a person to be able to both better understand and fit into a globalized world. We will benefit as a country if our future leaders meet and interact with people from many countries and many cultures. Unfortunately these students are far from typical. From a 2010 report prepared by the Institute of International Education, they state: "Just over one percent of all U.S. students enrolled in U.S. higher education at any academic level typically study abroad during any single academic year. Among students pursuing Bachelor's degrees, about 14 percent study abroad at some point during their undergraduate programs."

I hope this book will encourage students, parents, faculty, and administrators to support and promote education abroad programs.

Perhaps a new set of expectations for our college graduates (at least those who intend to lead their chosen fields) is in order. For example, not only critical thinking, team building, communication skills, and solid ethics are needed, but a global perspective may be the deciding factor for hiring a recent graduate. To gain such a perspective, students may want to consider adapting "new global strategies". For starters, here are a few recommendations:

Never let your age get larger than the number of countries you have explored.
Volunteer to work in a culture different from your own.
Learn to think through what life would be like in *their* shoes.
Learn both good and bad lessons from the cultures that you have explored.
Learn how to implement these good lessons into your personal and/or work life.

If you are a parent or grandparent, help your kids with these recommendations. Take them on a trip; pay for a trip; volunteer with them. Start getting them to "think globally". It is a very good investment in their future happiness.

For more information concerning the book and the importance of international education, contact:

Donald Gogniat, dag1@psu.edu, 717-891-7472

Book Club Thoughts

Why Toothbrush People is a Good Book for Book Clubs

- ✓ People will read it. This will be the only time when ALL members will have read the entire book.

- ✓ The information is useful and thought provoking for parents who are thinking about what their kids should do in college.

- ✓ The stories show how things change over time and the impact of certain events.

- ✓ The stories and photos have a spontaneous quality that lets the reader appreciate the possibility of finding experiences worth remembering anywhere.

Possible Questions for Discussion

- ✓ Who do you identify with; if you had written one of these stories which one do you think would have been yours?

- ✓ Are there any patterns that you can identify from the stories?

- ✓ What thing surprised you from the stories?

- ✓ Do the stories help to justify the role of an international experience as an important part of the college curriculum?

- ✓ Do you see any gender differences with the stories?

- ✓ How were long term memories (2004 and 1990) different from the 2010 stories? Which ones from 2010 do you think will have a lasting impact?

- ✓ Do you think Chapter Four makes sense, and have you ever taken the time to file away senses associated with happy moments?

- ✓ Do you have your own type of toothbrush person?

- ✓ Will you have a toothbrush person after reading this book?

A Dedication to Robbie Engelmann

Sometimes you know when you are around great people. They don't have to say much, you just have to watch them interact with others to appreciate their care and concern. So it was with Robbie Engelmann. No matter what the situation, Robbie conveyed a sense of "we are all in this together and let's affirm each other's potential and kindness". In fact one of her academic areas of expertise was forgiveness. She taught people to forgive and let go.

Having sailed twice on Semester at Sea as a faculty member with her husband and scholar Armin Rosencranz, she influenced many young students to deeply appreciate the opportunity to meet and learn from the people they encountered in all of the countries visited.

Cancer took her life too early and cheated others from learning and perhaps developing her kind attitude and love of life. It is certainly fitting that a book about special people (these toothbrush people) should be dedicated to the good works and memory of Robbie Engelmann.

Table of Contents

Chapter One

Introduction

I have a coffee cup that has printed on it, "We don't remember the days, we remember the moments". This book is about moments. For some reason, the photographs of people shown in this book have made a significant impact on the person who has written the letter that follows the photo.

The photographs are individuals known as "toothbrush people" because whenever the person who wrote the letter brushes their teeth, he or she is reminded to think about what the person in the photograph is doing at that moment -wherever she may be.

This "concept" started as an easy way to have a quiz for students on an international educational experience called Semester at Sea. SAS is an around the world academic program sponsored by the University of Virginia. Every fall and spring a ship filled with approximately 650 college students sails around the world stopping in at least ten countries along the way. I occasionally teach a course called Global Studies, the one course (from about 75 offerings by 25 faculty members) that every student is required to take. In some ways it is the "academic glue" that binds the voyage together. After we leave India, we are about halfway around the world and deep down we all know that we are now heading home. This is a good time to make sure that we are reflecting on this incredible adventure. With a toothbrush in my hand, on the first class after India, I talk to the students about the fact that we are now on the way home but we still have five countries left to explore. By now they know that this is a life changing time and that they need to get the most from this fortunate experience. Here is a small portion of that lecture:

> *What are we actually doing?*
>
> *It is hard to keep this in perspective when you are part of this Fellini Movie called SAS. On the intercom you hear, "The Women's author trip leaves at 9am; the Dean's tour*

will go to the embassy at 7; meet in the union, we climb Table Mountain at 8am"

We are here (use globe to point to India)

Your friends and family are here.

Now think back to all of the sights and sounds and glimpses into people's lives that you have had from Nassau to here: the fisherman, the taxi driver, the waiter, the little kids, the college students, the person who bought you dinner but really couldn't afford it.

This is not really a Fellini movie. These people are still living and smelling and breathing and feeling right now. In fact it may be hard to remember that they are still there.

It is different after India.

And although it is sad in some ways, we are now going home. We are halfway around the world and we are heading back to our ordinary lives (not away) every hour. And I think it is important even right now as we head home to think what this voyage is doing to you. You know that you are doing something that 99.99 of the world will never do.

What will this trip do to you? Or better yet, what has this trip done to you so far.

You know things that you thought you would never learn: countries, places, songs, landforms, political leaders, etc. You also know or at least are starting to know that you are in a closed system; on a marble that we all depend on, and this thing called the world is an interdependent planet.

Now what should you want out of the rest of this trip? What kinds of memories so far have been important to you?

After India it is a different voyage...

We are going to have 4 people talk about this subject today and reflect on what has happened to them.

(Presentations)

After these short student presentations, I ask the students to write a one page paper on someone they have met that has made an impact on them. They are to think about where they were and why this person left such an indelible memory.

When they are done writing their one page, they are asked to fold the paper in half and then in half again and to write their home address in the middle of this blank section on the back of the letter. I collect these papers and as proof they were in class, this "quiz" gives them a few points toward their final grade. I also explain that I will mail these letters back to them approximately one year later.

Sooner or later someone will ask what the toothbrush is for that I have been waving around for the entire lecture. That question will make for a lifelong memory for some of them. I tell them that from now on the person that you have just written about will be their "toothbrush person", and every time you brush your teeth - from now on – whenever your toothbrush touches your mouth, and you look into the mirror as you are brushing - you will be prompted to think, "I wonder how (and what) my *toothbrush person*" is doing today – right now?"

This little book is a compilation of "toothbrush people" through time. Students wrote these letters in 1990, 2004, and 2010. The book, therefore, is really two main sections of how these personal interactions have both affected them and how they have endured over time.

Finally, you don't have to travel around the world to have a toothbrush person, and the last section of the book will let you know how you too can become involved.

Chapter Two

2010 Letters

The second section of this book is a short collection of some of the "quizzes"/letters of students who have traveled around the world on Semester at Sea in the spring of 2010.

My initial contact with these students after the voyage in relation to this collection is an email as follows:

April 17rd, 2011

Hi Patrick,

I'm finally getting around to working on putting together a "Toothbrush" book. You have been selected as a possible entry for this book. The selection was based on several people who have read the letters and thought yours was particularly interesting or compelling. Additionally you had indicated that you have a photo of the person you have described in the letter – your toothbrush person.
The book will probably be developed into four sections. They are:

Section 1 will include an introduction to the concept of toothbrush person, and how it fits with SAS. We will also explain how the idea can be used to recall memories in any situation. At most this section will be five pages.

Section 2 will be the main portion of the book. Here we will have a photo on one page, and on the opposite page, the written letter. This appears to be 20 or so letters. That would make this section at least 40 pages.

Section 3 will be toothbrush letters from people on previous voyages. These voyages took place in 1990, and 2004. I will try and get in touch with people from these voyages to see if they still remember their toothbrush person. I would assume that a maximum of 20 pages or 10 stories from each voyage may be possible.

Section 4 will be ways to use the toothbrush concept in your daily life. This will include several short stories relevant to the concept. This section would be no longer than 5-10 pages.

The total length of the book would be approximately 100 pages.

I'm not sure who will want to publish the book yet, and I don't want to make ANY money from this project; but I think we can pull it off simply because it looks like it would be a nice publication (and a fun thing to set on a coffee table).
If you want to be part of the book and expect absolutely no financial reward for your participation, email me the photo of your toothbrush person (dag1@psu.edu) and I'll start putting the book together - slowly. I will make sure you are given credit for your part in the book. I am also mailing this same letter to your home address via regular mail just to make sure you are contacted.
I hope your life is going well. If you are ever in South-central Pennsylvania, say hello. My number is 717-891-7472. Also, please feel free to call or email if you have any questions about the book.

Thanks Fellow Adventurerrrs,
Don Gogniat
dag1@psu.edu

Since the 2010 students are the most recent entries, we still do not know whether they are in fact thinking about these "toothbrush people" whenever they brush their teeth. I suspect, however, that perhaps this is the time (tooth brushing) when images of their far away friends may pop into their minds every now and then. To momentarily drift back to the time and place of the chance meeting for the two of them, early in the morning as you are getting ready for the day, is probably a good experience when it happens. I hope that the bond established, no matter how strong, increases a spirit of "we are all in this together – it is nice to have known you. I hope you are well."

Here are twenty-two letters of the toothbrush people from a few students of the spring 2010 voyage. The entries are in alphabetical order.

2010 Photographs & Student Letters

Greta Bushnell, Spring 2010

I met Veena at the SOS Children's village in India. After the performance the children put on, Veena came up and asked if I would like to see her home. She was wearing a beautiful purple top and long skirt. When I told her I liked it she said "thank you" with a huge smile. She told me about her mom and brothers and sisters that lived in her house. The village puts about 10 kids together with a mom so they can grow up with the "family feeling". Her house was very nice and she made sure I met her mom.

She later told me that in 2011 her mother would retire and she was going to be very sad by this. She will still get to see her mom, but she will have an "aunt" live with her. I saw pictures of her past brothers and sisters who had gone off to get married and one who was getting her MBA. She spoke very proudly of them. As we spent time walking around the village, I got to meet Veena's friends and siblings. She was so excited for me to meet them.

A group of children were playing in an open area, but she wanted to keep walking around with me. Her English was very good but at times I wished I had been able to understand her better. I gave her some hair clips before I left and told her to share them with her friends and sisters. I wished that I had brought more with me. I told her that I would send her a letter when I got home and her face lit up.

I sat on the bus and waved to her through the window. She didn't take her eyes off me as I sat there. When the bus pulled away she smiled beautifully and waved goodbye. I cannot wait to send her a letter with a picture of the two of us.

Amy DeVillez, Spring 2010

I don't even know how to pronounce her name, but it sounded like Seraina. She didn't speak or understand English nor did I Khmer. The first time I met her I felt her hand grab mine before I even saw her face. Seraina picked me out of a crowd of 100 people visiting that orphanage, where she lived. I don't know why she chose me or why she became so affectionate so quickly, but immediately I fell in love with her.

We ran as fast as we could to where there were bracelets and rings. I bought a bracelet for me and a ring for her. She then grabbed my hand again and showed me her cubby and the unfortunate place she slept..... but only I knew it was unfortunate, because Seraina knew nothing more. I saw pictures she had drawn and the small amount of things she owned, which fit into a tiny bag. I felt embarrassed that my bag I brought to the orphanage for those few hours was bigger than her bag, which contained her whole life. After, we went down to play. It was so rewarding and interesting trying to figure out what was going on in their games. I kept losing and had no idea why! I didn't care though because every time I lost, Seraina laughed, which made me laugh too! I eventually caught on and we sat and played for awhile. We then had to leave too soon. Seraina walked me to the gate and wouldn't let go of me. Although not once during our time together did we ever verbally communicate, I could tell her eyes were begging me to stay. I looked back at her wishing I could stay and knowing she could read that in my eyes as well. We hugged over 10 times before I gave her some gifts I had brought (hats, pencils, mardi gras beads) and finally, we were torn away from one another.

It was the first time on this trip tears streamed down my face and I felt something I had never felt before. It wasn't something I could describe because although it was not a bad feeling, it was not a good one either. After a hour and a half and not being able to speak to each other, I felt a deeper connection with Seraina than some of the people I have known for years. I still wonder about her...what she is doing, what her life will be like, and if I will ever get to hold her. All I know is that little girl at the orphanage will be a special part of my heart and what she made me feel in the little time knowing each other is something I will always cherish.

Elena Favaro, Spring 2010

Her name was Sary. I met her the morning I went to Angkor Watt to see the sunrise. She was trying to sell me things, bracelets and postcards, just like all the other girls; but this one in particular, Sary, I promised her I would be back in the afternoon.

Going on about my day, I had forgotten about the promise and went on being a tourist. Leaving Angkor Watt for the last time, we walked back down the same dirt road to our bus. All these young girls swarmed us. Some told me they liked my earrings, so I took them right off and gave them to her. Then I saw Sary. I remembered my promise, but it seemed like she had thought about it more. She wrote me a letter telling me how beautiful I was and gave me her e-mail. I just started to cry. She tried to give me presents, but I could not accept them, until she told me it was okay.

My trip leader urged us to get on the bus. Tears flowing, I took the letter and got on the bus but she stood outside my window just smiling at me. She didn't want anything, she just smiled. As our bus started to pull away, I handed her a note with my e-mail saying I would never forget her. At this point she was running alongside our bus and handed me her school photo. I felt helpless, and the only thing I could offer was some money. Running alongside our bus she took the scarf off her neck and threw it into the bus window. "Never forget me" she yelled.

This is a story about a girl named Sary, a girl who had nothing, but gave me everything.

Kayla Howell, Spring 2010

My experience was incredible, just like you. I went to your orphanage and played downstairs, unaware you'd be able to hear me. I walked up the stairs, did you hear that? I walked up the stairs. I came into your room and saw you there and knew you were special from the start. I came to your side and lay near you unaware of your capabilities. I learned your age and found out that you were 11. You were 11 and so smart. You were so smart and were forced to lay there on your mat surrounded by infants, other children unable to communicate the way you could. You took a camera and I saw for the first time what life was like from your perspective. I saw the world from your beautiful brown eyes. I cried and held back tears and left the room, not because I wanted to leave you, but because I was angry. Angry a smart, beautiful 11 year old could be forced to stay on a mat all day long, all year long. Your legs and body may have been mangled and small, but they were woven together like a beautiful masterpiece. I came back to the room and touched your frail legs and I never wanted to let go. I wanted you to know I was there and know that you were beautiful. You blew me a kiss and I had to leave. I realized the privilege I had the next day as I danced at a spiritual dance. I got up from you and walked away that afternoon, but never wanted to forget how special you were. You have changed me and I don't even know your name. You have changed me and your face will remain.

YMCA Orphanage Village with the disabled youth, Vietnam, 2010.

Sarah Hudson, Spring 2010

When in Cambodia, we did a really quick stop at the Palm Tree Orphanage. While there, I met a little girl who was about 11 as well as a young boy. I didn't know what to expect when we arrived at the orphanage, but as soon as we walked in, we were greeted immediately with hugs and screams from all children of different ages. I noticed the boy at first standing really close to me, but he wasn't saying anything. I began to walk with him and he gave me a tour of the orphanage using few words. Soon after, a girl came up to me so excited to talk. She told me all of the things to buy, a rain hat, a bag, a ring, and a pencil case. I put on all my items and we all took a picture together. I didn't realize until after that the boy had jumped out of the picture at the last second. Now that I look back on that, I feel like that boy represented the apprehensiveness that I felt in coming to the orphanage. It was like a stop for us just to look at the lives of the children, but for them this was real life. The girl was happy to sing and play games, treating the visit as a play date, but now it seems as though the boy was almost tired of playing with the random people coming to observe his home. And I don't blame him one bit for that. It was a really eye opening to see the orphanage and meet the kids, but I hope next time I will have a way to make a difference rather than to just be an observer.

Richard Luck, Spring 2010

The person who left one of the most lasting impacts on me so far was my moped driver in Vietnam. He took Scottie and me in a back alley at 12:30 in the morning to get pho. We sat with three drivers for hours. We talked about life. We drank beer. We laughed. We asked them about the Vietnam War. One had fought for the Vietcong the other for the U.S. for South Vietnam. They had been in a "war" against each other 20 years ago. Now they were sitting by a cart with two Americans - people from the country that had changed and ruined their life. One raised his pant leg. His foot had been blown off. He pointed at it and said war. How could these people allow Scottie and me in their life? And genuinely be our friends. It was incredible. We asked them what they thought of Americans. The all said "We <u>love</u> Americans." Why? Why don't we feel like that towards them? Why when we hear Vietnam we literally <u>hate</u>, but they <u>love</u>? They told us without Americans they would have no house, no money, nothing. They said everything around them was because of Americans and their money. For as much as Scottie and I were intrigued by them, they were just as intrigued by us. They wanted to know why we were there. If we liked it. What were our feelings on Obama. The three men were incredible to open up their hearts to Americans and truly be able to forgive is something I hope I will take from them and have with me throughout the remainder of my life. If they have it in their hearts to be able to forgive us for what we did to them, may I find it in mine to forgive as well. This is only one of many events on this voyage that has truly impacted my life. Richard, don't forget any of them. Remember every day the children in Cambodia. Remember your want and need to help them. Follow your heart. Do what you love. Help where you can and never, ever forget, I know you won't.

Jessica Marshall, Spring 2010

My first day in Chennai, 3 friends and I met up to go out to explore. At the front gate, we were bombarded by tons of rickshaw drivers and honestly we just randomly picked one and got in and agreed on what I still can't get over – a ridiculously cheap fare. Our driver's name was Nana. He's married with a little 1 year old boy and his wife is pregnant with a child on the way (3 months, I believe). Anyway, he took us to a temple and we got there and tried to pay and be on our way but he told us, no, no I will stay here and wait. He continued to wait around for us the entire day and then took us to his house. We met his whole family and saw his house. It was then that it struck me how impoverished he and these Indian people are. I had a rough time through that whole first day with the massive amounts of people and dirt and germs (I'm a germ-a-phobe) but once I got back to the ship that night, I had never been so thankful for what I had. I'm not just saying that either, I was/am truly thankful. The meal I had that night on the ship, I didn't leave one bite behind and when I laid in my bed that night I sat there awake so grateful for even having a clean bed with blankets and a pillow. Coming home from experiencing India, I know I'm a changed person – and I can definitely say it is for the better. I knew SAS was going to be an experience, but nothing could have ever prepared me for this.

Kelly Mertens, Spring 2010

Samya was 12 years old and she didn't want to play or talk. She just wanted to hug, and be touched. She reminded me of all the kids at the shelter in DC, the ones who just will crawl in your lap because they don't get enough physical reminders of love. I didn't give her the bag that I wanted to, though, how I wish I did. I felt so awkward with her, like I should be doing more with her, talking or making her laugh, but all she needed was to be held. She told me not to cry when we left and I kept that promise. I just locked it away, though I wondered if she would have felt more care about if I had. She lived in conditions that I would call a camp. I hope she is learning and growing and I hope she knows that she is beautiful. I hope she gets hugs at least once a day and that she'll finally get a bag. I hope she knows she's loved. Remind her.

Christina McQuire, Spring 2010

While in Japan, I visited the city of Hiroshima. It was an emotional day – seeing the "A-bomb dome" that is still standing, visiting the children's memorial, and spending time walking through the museum. After I had gone through the museum, I decided to walk through the Hiroshima Peace Park and spend some time in reflection. I heard a beautiful voice singing in Japanese. It was coming from a middle-aged woman sitting on a park bench. I sat down on the bench next to her and listened to her song as I gazed around the beautiful park.

I was filled with a sense of peace. It was hard not to feel a sense of peace – the entire Hiroshima memorial was focused on peace. Instead of focusing on war and blame and the atrocities that had happened, the memorial was about world peace and what could be done to achieve it.

I smiled at the woman next to me and she smiled back with warmth. As she finished her song, I continued to look at her and said "hello" to her in Japanese. She came over to me beaming and put her hands on my face. She said "hello" back to me and then kissed me on the cheek. She pulled some candies out of her bag, graciously offered them to me, and gave me a hug before she went back to her bench and began another song.

This woman epitomized the meaning of the Memorial and the emotions behind it. She showed me the true meaning of peace and gave me a glimpse of what a peaceful world could look like. I don't know her name, and I don't know a thing about her life, but I often wonder if she is back on that park bench, bringing peace to others as she brought to me.

Michael Moore, Spring 2010

My toothbrush person is a young Indian girl of about 2 years old that I met 2 days ago in the backwaters of Kochi. Everyone we met in the village was so curious of the American tourists, but the innocence of the young girl's eyes gave me chills. As the mother held her most prized possession in her arms for us to admire, it made me think of the importance of family, a human unity in the world. I stared back into her crystal like brown eyes and wondered what her future will be. Will she go to school? Will she live in the village forever? Will she live past the age of five? Will she live to be a great grandmother? In an area with so much poverty, her mother had adorned her child with earrings, anklets, and other small jeweled items to show the love she had. It made me wonder why people take family and love so for granted. No words were exchanged in the brief contact, but as I held the little girl's hand, I wanted to know what she was thinking. She has a whole future waiting ahead of her to grow, to form her values, to make connections with people, places and things. What kind of person will she grow up to be? It made me reflect, what are the experiences in my life that have molded me into who I am today? More importantly, who am I today? Who will I be tomorrow? In one year, when I receive this letter, what will I have accomplished? How can I make this little girl's life better? Will I have made someone's life better since meeting her? The world is full of opportunities to make people happy, and yet they are often overlooked. We are all human, we have the same chemical makeup, the same feelings and worries, yet we often forget and only look at the differences. So Mike, if you have not done so yet today, go make someone happy.

Sarah Nininger, Spring 2010

I walked into the orphanage and instantly saw a young woman holding a boy who looked to be no older than six. He had a severely painful cleft lip and palate. His arms were nothing but little stumps with 2 fingers on each one.

The young woman placed him on the floor where we then saw that his legs weren't usable as they were tangled in every direction possible. I found myself uncomfortable to acknowledge his presence and basically spent too much time avoiding him. I don't know how it happened, when or why it happened, but next thing I knew I was sitting with him in my lap.

Together we were coloring a McDonald's picture. I underestimated this young man. He was 12 years old and has become part of my everyday life so far. I find myself to be embarrassed thinking about how naïve and ignorant I was when I first saw him. When I left the orphanage, he grabbed my St. Mary's charm and kissed it and then hugged me goodbye.

Sandy Noel, Spring 2010

"I found myself"

In December, 2008, my mother passed away to colon cancer. During that whole process, I was strong enough to be there for my dad and my sister. Yet, I felt that a huge part of me had died. The fact that I can no longer hear her voice or call her to tell her about something I did really hurt me. After her death, I realized that I was more attached to my mom than anyone. I wondered how was I ever going to move forward in life?

While I was in Chennai, India, I went on a SAS trip to an orphanage called Bala Mandir. Families who don't have enough to support their kids leave their kids there to be taken care of by a group of wonderful men and women who feed them, educate them, and help provide aide for college/jobs for them. I was blessed to have met this lady named Girlija. Girlija lost her husband 15 years ago. She was telling me how she honestly didn't know how else she was supposed to live without him. Rather than live a life of sorrow, dwelling on her husband's death, she decided to serve those who couldn't serve themselves. She partnered with the orphanage and she mentors the kids (mainly the older girls) and cooks lunch/dinner for them. When she told me her story, I began to realize that I can do so much for myself. Girlija told me that the only way to succeed (after the death of a loved one) is to "continue to live the way they would have wanted you to live."

I came on this trip with SAS to find myself because I lost myself when my mom died. And here I am in India getting genuine advice from someone who managed to make it through her struggles. Girlija really helped me find myself. In years to come, I hope to make a difference in the lives of others just as she did for me.

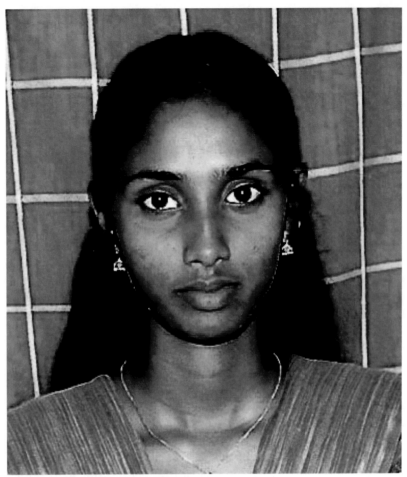

Caitlyn Sue O'Flaherty, Spring 2010

Can I do this on one side of one page? Can I tell you about beautiful, about impoverished, about unprecedented openness, about selflessness as an intrinsic quality, as a way of life...can I tell you about Emi Buela? Can I tell you that she is still there, in that one room home—because it was home, in every important sense of the word—and I wish I could be there too. She lived along a row, in a building with no door. There was one bed, immediately to the left when you walked inside. There was a sort of icebox, a sewing table, a cracked television, and, behind a curtain, a bookshelf full of papers and knick knacks and old, dry flowers. Five people lived there: Emi, her brother Jacob, her parents, and her grandmother. I'd met her on the street outside, while I walked aimlessly through Chennai, in a glorious daze of sensory overload and smiling. I was in her neighborhood, a slum by every technical definition, when she came right up to me. She spoke English well, though I had to speak slowly to help her understand me. She invited me into her home after some small talk and we sat on her bed goofing off and trading questions like candy. When I asked her what she did for fun, she pulled out a big sheet of wood that was like some kind of combined checkerboard pool table. It had a hole in every corner. She had a box of checkers and proceeded to organize them into two stacks in the middle. We flicked one checker toward the stacks to break them and start the game, at which time I discovered I was terrible. We played for over an hour. Then there was some kind of miscommunication where it was somehow decided that I wanted to dance. I decided to go with it as Emi ran over to a cracked radio. Like a wave the music picked us up and turned the home into a dance party, all of us flailing around to Tamil songs and laughing like we were afraid we might never have another chance. I took Emi's mother's hands and did some old sixties sock hop moves I'd liked in middle school. Suddenly, more faces appeared in the doorway and the whole neighborhood flooded in. That tiny room had 15 or 16 happy dancing friends, moving together in the sweaty heat of an Indian afternoon. It was magic. Once we'd worn ourselves out and filtered the crowd back down to some semblance of Emi's family, we split two popsicles amongst us all (see, it was all they had, and they offered it all, without hesitation). We watched a scratched up video of the first James Bond on a that tiny, wonderful screen, and dramatically acted out the fight scenes. Emi kept a diary with a series of surveys she'd given her friends (much like the kind of question answer pages I used to write up when I was little all the time). The questions were like—favorite food, dress, music, film, friend, god, most unforgettable day, and my favorite, definition of a friend. Many surveys had been filled out in Tamil, and when I couldn't read it, Emi would do her best to translate the responses. I was struck by the number of definitions that said "greatest gift from god," (no matter what god they were referring to). She had me fill out a survey, and then she showed me hers. She went to the spot for "most unforgettable day," crossed out her previous answer, and wrote today. She looked into my eyes like they were going to tell her answers to important questions like why do we live worlds apart? or do we really? like I was someone she would not forget. I promised her I would never forget her, but she went ahead and reminded me not to 18 or so more times. I wish she'd had an email, or a mailing address, something. I wish she'd had a computer. She wants to study software engineering; she wants to travel the world. She's never left this side of Chennai. To see such dreams flourish in her world was inspiring—the kind of inspiring that makes me sure I will find ways to reach my goals, to make a difference for the phenomenally beautiful people I have met. I have such opportunity. I am so lucky, to already have the means to pursue my dreams, to satiate my wander lust, to have been there, in India, dancing with Emi Buela. I want these things for her. This was one of a hundred most unforgettable days. A scarlet, dusty sunset, tucked me in that night, thinking of Emi. So look back at this, future self; take none of it for granted. Life is now. Every minute. Nanbu ("Friends in Tamil") are everything.

Graham Quinn, Spring 2010

I don't know his name. I don't know his age. I don't know much about him, but in Chennai, India, near the colorful Hindu temple, I met a man who tried to sell me a drum. I didn't want the drum, but he was persistent. He followed me down the street, continually asking how much the drum would need to cost for me to buy it. I didn't want to just brush him off so I asked him his name to side track him. He said it, and then asked where I was from and if I was in school. I answered, asked him similar questions, and he told me he was Muslim, couldn't afford school, and he just sold drums. After talking a while longer, I began to realize that yes he's poor but so what. We talked in the same way I would talk to my roommate at school. He wasn't different at all aside from his skin color and language, of course. I could have been looking in the mirror. So I ask myself, in a world that seems to me to be getting smaller every day, why do we live in fear of what is unknown, different, or strange? For when we take the time to look past appearance, we ultimately end up looking at the familiar, even ourselves sometimes. I have learned that it's not what you do, but who you do it with that makes experiences... memories. I hope in 1 year I feel and act the same way!

Laurel Rose, Spring 2010

I can't stop crying. I have never felt this much emotion in my life. I didn't want to leave India – I couldn't. The face of this old, beautiful woman won't leave my thoughts. We didn't even speak. She just held me, kissed me, and smiled. She had no teeth, but she had the happiest smile I have ever seen. She was sitting outside of the ship with a few other Indians. She was selling peacock feathers and other miscellaneous goods but she just gave me the feathers because she felt what I felt, I think. The night before we left I had met her. I didn't think I would ever see her again, but there she was right before I got on the ship. I was almost late because I couldn't stop hugging her and holding her hand. I asked the others about her and they said she didn't have a home and she was a very old grandmother. When I walked away, one of my favorite souls on this ship (Lindsay) and I started balling our eyes out. We couldn't leave her. When I go back to the U.S., things will be so different. All these people I have met will be with me forever. Kenzi in Vietnam, Nick from the orphanage in Cambodia, and all the smiling faces on and off the ship. I truly see into the soul of everyone I meet and Semester at Sea has already impacted me in ways that I can't even explain my gratitude for. Thank you to #1 my FAMILY, friends, this earth and its beautiful people

Alicia Sherrin, Spring 2010

I met this young woman in the dining area of a hotel in Siam Reap, Cambodia. She was sitting in the corner of the dining area playing a traditional instrument. She looked very sad and lonely, so I went up to talk to her.

I learned a few phrases in Khmer, the language of Cambodia, from my guide, Thy, so I said to this woman, "Suicidai! Danit chmo awai?" which means "Hello! What's your name?" She looked back at me with wide eyes and it took her a moment to collect herself and respond. I feel terrible because I can't remember her name now. I should have written it down...

I replied "Chmoro baknion ge Liza" (My name is Alicia) and then I pointed to her instrument and asked "What is it?" "Sikhon" she replied.

I told her "Kinhom jochat skihon!"

At this point she grasped my hand, caressed my arm and stared deeply into my eyes, into my soul.

"I like you," she exclaimed, "I really like you!"

I was touched by this and I meekly replied "Acon, I like you, too" with a smile on my face.

She started to shake her head in a gesture of "No, you don't understand." At this point, little language was used but through a mixture of gestures, she got her point across. For two years she had worked there, playing sikhon for tourists in this resort. Never in that entire time had someone come up and spoken Khmer to her. Not even a simple "Suicidai."

I felt so sad. She was so kind, so sweet and no tourist had ever reached out to her. Never again will I be able to travel and just see the sights. I must engage with the people, with their language, their lifestyle.

I wonder how she is doing now. If anyone else has talked to her? If she is happy?

Emily Smullin, Spring 2010

I visited an orphanage while we were in Cambodia. A little girl ran up to me and hugged me and didn't want to let go. She was 12 years old and had lived at the orphanage for her whole life. She was full of life and seemed to be one of the happiest little girls despite all she had been through. She showed me around her home and where they slept and went to class. We bonded through playing hand games and she taught me songs that they enjoyed singing together. When it came time to leave, she held onto me tight and begged me not to leave. She wanted me to stay the night with her. When I told her I couldn't she started crying. This little girl touched my heart on so many levels! She has been emailing me, so we have been able to stay in touch and I was able to send her pictures of the two of us from my visit. The opportunity to have met this girl opened my eyes to wanting to help orphans in the future. I will definitely never forget this experience and hope to see her one day again!

Sarah Ward, Spring 2010

I went on an independent trip with my friend Mike in India. We went to Dehli, Agra, and Jaipur. We had a tour guide in Agra that took us to the Taj Mahal and a few other places. His name was hard to pronounce, but he told us to call him Hustad. The two of us had a few chances to talk about our differences. He asked me what kind of man I wanted to marry, and it really made me think. By the time I finished telling him, I knew the person I had been dating was not right for me. Crazy how a Muslim tour guide in India was able to open my eyes to that. We continued to share stories and joke the rest of the day. He called me Princess the whole day, because he said I was pretty. Two days after we left him, he called our driver and asked to speak to us. He said he was back at the Taj Mahal and was thinking about us. He gave us his card so we can add him on facebook and email him. I hope we can keep in touch.

Melissa Wergland, Spring 2010

In India, my rickshaw driver invited me and my friends to come meet his family. We agreed and we walked down a narrow alleyway to get to his house. Many people came out of their houses and began waving and smiling. All of their doors and windows were open to keep the house a little cooler because there was no air conditioning. I heard singing coming from the distance and the rickshaw driver, Salim, said it was people praying at the mosque.

As I continued to walk, there were many smiling faces lined up outside all to see us. We entered his family's house and it had only three beds and a small room to cook in. The walls and floor were cement. There was one dresser and no furniture, TV, or computer. The small house was bare. We met his wife, mother, and two small children. Pretty soon all of the neighbors were filling up inside of his house.

A girl ran over to me and handed me some beautiful bangles. She said that she wanted me to have them. I gave her my fan from China in return. She invited me to her house. We went over there and I met her mother and her sister. Her mother served me tea. This girl's name was Sumaiya. She showed me her jewelry and gave me a pair of her earrings. I told her I felt bad and she said, "No, I want you to have them because we are friends now." That moment touched my heart. She barely had anything yet she was giving me her few things she had. We went shopping later on and we got matching bangles. She also put henna on my hand and her mom gave me some dinner. We decided we will be pen pals. It was amazing to feel the connection with someone so different, yet so much alike.

Ashley Withers, Spring 2010

I can't remember her name, but she saved me. Met her at the bus station in Viet Nam and she was the only nice person I had met all day. My nerves were fried and I was standing nervously in the middle of the station looking around with a confused look. She came up to me and in broken English tried to translate my ticket for me and point me in the right direction. I still had 30 minutes to wait for my bus and miraculously it was the same bus she was on, so she sat with me. She offered to get me snacks for the ride and when a few beggars came over to me she sent them away. We didn't get to sit next to each other on the bus. My 3 ½ hour bus ride that consisted of 6 people crammed into a "bus" the size of a minivan and had me seated next to a man who urinated himself, his wife and a small child with severe motion sickness. Halfway through our trip we stopped at a rest stop and she came back to where I was seated to see if I was alright. I replied shakily that I was OK and she told me to wait right there. She returned 5 minutes later with some yogurt and she told me that it would make me feel a lot better. When we finally arrived back in Ho Chi Minh she made sure I knew where I was going and then she headed back to her university, but not before I surprised her with a huge hug. Her kindness and complete willingness to go out of her way for me was like nothing I've ever seen before. I owe her my safety and complete gratitude and yet she never asked for anything in return.

Jay Yoder, Spring 2010

I was south of Kochi about 2 ½ hours (bus ride) in a small beach town called Alleypay Backwaters. Later that night our chef and captain took us inland to a small village. We entered the back of a shack. After a few minutes drinking the local coconut beer, four to five Indian men sat at our table to join us for drinks. They then began creating some of the most beautiful music my ears have ever heard. One of the men was a singing teacher and his voice almost brought tears to my eyes. The rest of the men used the table as instruments, banging their knuckles and fingers so fast I could hardly keep up. After many songs they asked us to sing one. Never being one to show off my bad voice, I began to sing Bob Marley's <u>Three Little Bird's On My Doorstep</u>. They smiled and hummed the tune with huge smiles. I also taught them <u>Iron Man</u> which was a hit. The teacher started to teach me a singing lesson and I couldn't keep up, but he kept on me "again – again" he would say. He then told everyone to be quiet and told me to try. I did the whole lesson in Hindu just like he taught and everyone started in applause and shaking my hand and yelling with excitement. I never felt love like that, I never had a teacher like that, and I never had human connections like that. The teacher and I, hand and hand, said our goodbyes and thanks with a perfect end to a perfect night.

Patrick Young, Spring 2010

In Phnom Pehh, I had the fortunate opportunity of meeting Mr. Chum Mey. This man, a man of probably 70 years of age, was sitting by himself on a solitary bench in the middle of the Tuol Sleng Genocidal Complex. After talking with my tour guide for a bit, he informed me that this very lonely man who was sitting by himself only visits Tuol Sleng on rare occasions. He also informed me that out of the 20,000+ people who were victimized at the Tuol Sleng Center, this gentleman was one of the three survivors. After slowly making my way over to this gentleman, I proceeded to sit next to him on this otherwise small bench. He hesitantly and shyly glanced at me and then stood up to walk away. As I watched him leave, he slowly turned around and waved me on to follow him.

Though Mr. Mey spoke only Khmer and I spoke only English, this language barrier did not lessen my experience or our connection. Mr. Mey showed me around the genocidal holding center, his previous home for over 2 years. He showed me his cell where he was cuffed and beaten. He showed me the torture devices the Pol Pot's followers used on him and his friends. He showed me his blood on the ground, his finger nail scratches in the sides of his wooden cell.

At the end of my visit, Mr. Chum Mey showed me his picture on the wall, a picture of him and a few other buddies who had perished in the Cambodian genocide. He then reached in and gave me the absolute tightest hug I've ever experienced. I could feel this man's pain, his anguish. To this day, I still think about him constantly. I wonder how Mr. Mey, a man of so few words, is reconciling the atrocities that he witnessed. Meeting this man was life-changing and I now know it is my job to inform people of the otherwise overlooked genocide that occurred in Cambodia.

Chapter Three

Long Term "Toothbrush Person" Memories

The second portion of this book deals with people who have remembered their toothbrush person over time.

Dr. Robert Weigl, Ph.D. has studied the effects of the Semester at Sea experience on student participants through a detailed longitudinal research project. In a recent report he says:

"From my informants' comments, supplemented by my own program experience, I want to suggest that there are seven lines along which SAS students are likely to develop. In order of their approximate prominence in respondents' comments to me, these seven developmental lines are:

1. Development of world travel skills.
2. Interpersonal development.
3. Cognitive-intellectual development.
4. Motivational-vocational development.
5. Identity development.
6. Intercultural development.
7. Moral development.

I believe further research will reveal the following: that students may move much further along one development line than another; that students will contrast in the clusters of developmental lines along which they grow; that many students can show enormous movement along one line—development of world travel skills—while showing almost no movement on another—intercultural development; that some areas of development do not emerge during the voyage, but continue to expand in the many years afterwards".

His research findings have shown that students really do need time to "digest" what has happened to them, and that many of his stated developmental lines "grow" long after the initial experience. In some ways this is similar to what the toothbrush person has meant to students over time. This section of the book explores these feelings. We will start with memories that are approximately eight years old – the 2004 student letters and/or stories.

2004
Letters and Comments

Katie (Roberts)Bortz, Spring 2004

Only 48 hours after leaving the country of India, the image of a particular face still remains vivid in my mind. My "toothbrush image" is of my home stay sister Bria. For the small fee of $25, I was taken into the heart and home of a family forever. However Bria, as well as the rest of the family, gave back to me more than I could have ever invested. Bria is 25 years old (3/04) & is an aspiring artist. She has never left her country of India, has never attended college, & lives the life of a traditional Indian woman. She possesses such grace, has perfectly full lips, and eyes as deep & full as the moon. Her humble demeanor, her servitude, and her Indian "head bob" are things I will never forget. She seems quite content with her life, yet as she waited for me to finish my meal before eating her own, or showed me her artwork, I sensed in her a longing – perhaps for her own adventure – for something a bit more than she now knows. It wasn't a material longing, but more sentimental. I see such tremendous potential in her, such exquisite and extraordinary generosity... as she patiently dressed me in a Sari, filled my hand with henna in the backseat of a car, or raced me to the mall to bargain for a pair of traditional Indian earrings. It is for all these memories, and for the life lessons she taught me, that I pierced my nose just like hers. Each day I look in the mirror, or someone asks me about my nose piercing, I will be able to tell the story & smile, & for a brief moment be brought back to these 3 wonderful days in India.

For me the toothbrush concept has been one that has waxed & waned out of my life. Perhaps this was not the overwhelming intent of the project, but for me, it has been a sort of grounding rod. I think we all go through times when life gets away from us. We are caught up in our jobs, our day to day life, our wants, our bills, our hard times….and we so easily forget those really really great moments in our life. For me, I'd have one of those hard days, those days when you didn't remember to appreciate much, or see the good in others, & then somehow, my SAS experience would find its way trickling back into my life. I'd be lucky enough to get an invitation to lunch at an Indian restaurant with a friend, or receive an email from a SAS companion, or have someone comment about my nose ring. Just that would be enough to make me bring out the photo albums, the journal I kept along the journey, or call an old friend and "re-charge" & get back to appreciating how rich & wonderful of a life I am fortunate enough to have. I think about Bria, & wonder what she is doing now: if she has more children, if she's still living with her parents, if she's had any artwork "make it." I wonder if she thinks of me.

I have not corresponded with Bria since I left India over 8 years ago (wow how the time flies) but believe I do this nostalgically every time my path crosses someone with the country of India in their blood.; their unforgettable head bob, their quiet and calm demeanor, their generosity. I engage in conversation, I smile & do what I can, to do the best for them in the situation I am in. I tell them about my time there, most are receptive & grateful for my interest in their country. I really think about where they have come from, what is must be like to be there, and now here, & how they get to be who they are. There are people in foreign countries, and others right in our own neighborhood, that lack something that we have in excess, not always money or things, but freedom and knowledge. Being on the more fortunate end gives us a duty to dispense what we have, what we know, what we have learned. To me that is the overarching lesson of the toothbrush person. Why do you remember who you remember – who you picked to be your toothbrush person? Maybe because they did something you can't ever forget, said something you'll always hear, or because they are constant force that grounds you.

Sharon Christ, Spring 2004

March 17, 2004 – enroute to Vietnam

There are too many faces melting together. There are the three women writers I met the first day in India...intelligent, accomplished, affluent, professional women, mothers, wives.

There are the faces at the temples in Kancheeporum – the old men sitting outside the temple, on the steps, dark and lined, observing us as much as we were observing them.

There are all the faces of Chennai – in the flower market, vegetable market, street vendors, rickshaw drivers, store managers, beggars, bus boys and the women in a store immediately outside the harbor.

And the faces in the Dalit village – students, shyly smiling, sneaking glances at us; the librarian and the teacher who wanted me to find them husbands when I went home; the director of Delta School, passionate about his vocation;

Lazarus, the consultant, who spent lots of time with me and all my questions; the villagers...smiling, anxious to see us, to be close, to touch us, to show us their life.

All these faces form a collage in my mind--all were welcoming, warm. The collage will remind me of strength in adversity, doing what they can with what they have and being most gracious as they do it. Brushing my teeth will take much longer from now on.

January, 2012 – York, PA

Eight years have passed and I'm sad to say that my life hasn't changed much although my thoughts have. I often think of my toothbrush persons. The picture I took of the librarian and teacher in the Dalit village sits on my desk in my office. I look at it often and I remember a simpler life. On my "bad" days, I look at it and remember my experiences at Semester at Sea. I wonder what that librarian and teacher are doing at that very moment. What is a "bad" day for them? How does it compare to mine? These thoughts always make my "bad" day better. I have shelter that is much more than mud and sticks, running water, electricity, a steady, well paying job, closets full of clothes, a car, an education. But who is happier with what they have? I know I can do with less – but I don't.

My job has evolved into being the international student contact on campus and guess who are my favorite international students? Yes, those from India. I feel I can relate to them. I share my experiences with them; I celebrate with them; I eat with them; I have become friends with them. I have dozens of families to visit now when I return to India (and I *will* return), people who are willing and anxious to share their lives with me. For that I am grateful. If it weren't for my toothbrush persons reminding me of a different time, a different place, a different life, my thoughts would still revolve around my everyday life in York, PA.

Andrew Gall, Spring 2004

The most memorable experience I had with host-country nationals during SAS took place in Japan. A few of my friends and I traveled to Kyoto independently on the first day we arrived in-country, and made the mistake of not booking a hotel or hostel ahead of time. When the evening came we wandered around town looking for affordable options, but every place we visited in our price range was already booked. As the sun set we walked around quite aimlessly considering what to do. We had no place to go. It was too late to take the train back to Osaka. We had no hotel options. We barely knew where we were. We decided that we'd look for a city park, hopefully with benches, and sleep there. And why not? There's no crime in Japan, and no homelessness, we were pretty sure. We'd surely be alright for one night. That was our decision. So as we were wandering through neighborhoods looking for a decent park to crash in, two young girls started to call to us from a driveway. "Hello." " How are you?" "What's your name?" they asked us. They were practicing their English, but weren't proficient yet. With nothing else to do at that moment, we decided to talk with them. We tried to ask them if they knew of any low-cost hotels that we could try. This line of questioning was beyond their comprehension level, so they went inside their house to get their father, who came out to chat with us in his also-limited English. Somehow we communicated to him that we had no place to sleep, and he seemed to want to help us. But the language barrier prevented us from getting into detail about how much we were willing to pay and what our exact plans were in Kyoto. So the father, the patriarch of the family, invited us all into his house while he looked for a solution to the language barrier. He picked up his phone and called his brother, who was proficient in English, and put us on the phone to explain our predicament. The brother could understand us pretty well, but his English wasn't fluent enough for us to communicate clearly, so it was decided that the he would come over to the house to talk to us in person. It was going to take 20 minutes for him to arrive, so we had some time to kill. We were invited to sit at the table in the family's living room to wait for our interpreter to arrive. So we sat down with the patriarch, his wife, their son, and their two daughters, the ones who had originally flagged us down on the street. And that's when the cultural exchange started. Although we didn't speak any Japanese and the family couldn't speak English, we introduced ourselves by name and started talking about our journey around the world on Semester at Sea. We made phonetic name tags so they could pronounce our names, and we drew pictures and maps of our adventures. The father explained to us that he was a business owner, his son worked for him part-time while attending college, and the daughters went to high school. After a few minutes somehow we forgot that we couldn't speak the same language, because we could communicate with each other on a basic level, a human level. When the English-proficient brother finally arrived, we explained our predicament in detail and told him about our lodging price range. He must have called 15 places on our behalf, always checking with us on whether the rate was acceptable or not. But none of them were. There was nothing available for under $100, and my friends and I were close to broke because Japan was the last country on our trip and incidentally the most expensive. We just couldn't afford to stay in Kyoto that night. But alas, there we were. Finally, the patriarch stopped the brother from calling hotels and explained to us that we were welcome to spend the night at his office downtown. The family had some foam mats, pillows, and blankets that they could lend us, although it would not be very luxurious, he explained. My friends and I all looked at each other in disbelief at the kindness of the offer. An hour earlier we were planning on sleeping on the ground in a random park in a strange city, and now we were being offered floor space in an office with fluffy pillows. Of course we accepted the offer. The patriarch's son was assigned to drive us to the office, make sure we were comfortable there, and of course he had to spend the night there with us because we were still strangers. As luck would have it, the family business was located in the commercial center of Kyoto, so the next morning we were already very close to all of the tourist sites that we planned to visit that day. We said thank you and farewell to the son who had driven us to the office and babysat us while we slept. I was so touched by the kindness of the Japanese family that went out of their way to help us find shelter that night in Kyoto. I will never forget how I felt about humanity; first that it existed, and second that people are people everywhere.

Leslie Gant, Spring 2004

Toothbrush person: *Calabra Favella Service Visit* – Tues. February 3rd, 2004:

"One of my most memorable days in Brazil was visiting the Calabar community, (located on the inner part of Salvador) to learn about urban poverty. It turned out to be more of a "show" than "tell". The streets resembled dilapidated/old movie sets with fake-looking storefront facades. All the locals looked pretty miserable. Men sat along stoops with somber faces & the woman looked emotionless, holding their grimy toddlers.

We arrived to the primary school & that too looked desolate *at first*. The few children I saw appeared timid to be in our presence, until I brought out my sketchbook and crayons. Within minutes the place was swarming with kids! Soon, children who did *not even attend* the school were running down the hills toward us, their parents hollering behind them the whole way! We had certainly made an impression, most likely because we had goodies and digital cameras. Out of all the children I saw, *one stood out...*

William was a polite, 7 year old Salvadorian boy with a sleeveless green shirt and a bright smile I'll never forget. Little did I know he was oozing with talent, too. I gestured for him to draw something in my sketchbook, and within minutes he had illustrated Mickey Mouse from head to toe, with impeccable detail! After autographing the picture, he brought my friend and me upstairs to a classroom void of inspiration & resources. There weren't any supplies in sight to cultivate William's creativity (or his peers). We tried to ask him questions about his dreams & aspirations, but the language barrier made it impossible to understand one another.

William broke our frustration by spontaneously performing the most insane dance moves I've ever seen – he was a Capoeira superstar! After my friend & I spent the rest of the afternoon bonding with this amazing boy, we decided to pool together our money to buy him some art supplies. We were determined to invest in his talents & that was the least we could do.

But suddenly, a sea of children surrounded us, yelling that our bus was waiting & it was time to leave! When we turned around, our little friend was nowhere in sight. We called out "Donde esta William!?" But nobody could find him. My friend and I reluctantly got on the bus. It broke my heart to leave without saying goodbye or giving him encouragement of some sort. It was like a dream – did that experience even happen? Yes- I have the Mickey Mouse illustration to prove it!

When I brush my teeth and I think of William, that sweet Brazilian boy oozing with creative talents & potential, I question what happened to him. What could his life become, if raised in a nurturing environment? What is he doing now, as he approaches young adulthood?

When I think of him, I'm reminded that it is not our *skills* that make us great. It's what we do with them that really counts. I hope to God he is able to put his to use for good… and that he's managed to keep his smile along the way.

Since that day in Brazil, I never want to let an opportunity pass to encourage someone or speak life to them… You never know when *or if* you'll see their face again.

Marie Gernes, Spring 2004

Tao found me in Ho Chi Minh City, on the steps of an old building in the central city. I remember it as a cathedral, with a huge staircase in front. I was waiting to meet a friend on the stairway to plan our afternoon in the city. This tiny boy with floppy brown hair skipped up the steps and sat down next to me, pointing at my camera and making funny faces. He spoke enough English to compensate for my complete ignorance of Vietnamese, and introduced himself as Tao, asked to play with my camera, and wanted to take pictures. Tao moved like he was full of light, like he didn't need to think to run.

I was in a daze. That morning, I had gone to the American War Museum, in part to pay respects as an American – not realizing that you can't pay for respect in a situation like that. I paid an entrance fee, paid for books sold by a veteran in the courtyard, paid what I thought I could as an American surrounded by pictures of devastated fields, starving children and murder. When my dad was just a few years older than I was on that day, he had lived outside Saigon in Army barracks as a helicopter pilot in the Vietnam War. We had Vietnamese art on our living room walls. He'd never made a big deal of his time there and didn't let it define his life, only showing me his slides the day before I left for SAS and saying what a beautiful country he'd seen. There was a helicopter in the museum's courtyard- this place was part of my history, too.

Tao found me later on those steps and stuck out his tongue, crossed his eyes for the camera, laughed when he saw the pictures on the screen. He made me smile too, then snuggled his head on my shoulder when he saw tears come to my eyes. When my friend Lacy met us, he took one of each of our hands and swung to jump down the steps, suspended between us. "Be careful," he told us several times. He took us through the market around the city, I don't remember exactly what we did all afternoon, but I remember that he kept smiling, asking to take pictures, pointing out parts of his city that we would never have noticed.

We stopped for an ice cream cone and Lacy and I took out our wallets to pay. Lacy's traveler's checks were gone. Tao didn't run away, he just looked around and put his hands in his pockets. "Be careful." In his pocket, I saw a wad of checks Tao was holding onto that he'd taken from Lacy's bag. He gave it back and said simply, "Sorry."

"Be careful," he said to us – I wish I could say we'd done the same for him. I know we bought him a meal, we asked if wanted anything, we gave him some money to take home – but in the end he left for home and so did we. I wish I would say that we'd both given him all of our cash, knowing we had a free meal on the ship and plenty of souvenirs already. I wish there was some way to start to even out our lives. Need was not an issue for us in the way it was for Tao. I remember that we weren't mad, but we both inexplicably felt hurt. How could we possibly have felt betrayed by someone we'd just met, by a child who clearly needed money more than we ever would?

When Don asked us to write our toothbrush letters in Core, I wrote about Tao and a woman I'd met in Lençois Brazil. I think of them both when I remember Semester at Sea for reasons that I think are different but complementary, mixed up in a way that reminds me of that time. I remember sharing absolute contentment with an older woman in Lençois, regret and sorrow with a small boy in Vietnam. And I remember feeling joy with people on opposite sides of this world.

Mary Hill, Spring 2004

I was not a student but was a Nurse Practitioner working to keep our students healthy during their voyage. However, I had the opportunity to learn right along with them. My Semester at Sea voyage changed my life, just as it did for every one of the students, faculty, and staff. When Dr. Gogniat made the toothbrush assignment in Global Studies, Lazar immediately came to mind.

I met Lazar while leading a group of Semester at Sea students for an overnight visit to a Dalit Village outside of Chennai, India. Our leader was Henry Thiagaraj, who was the founder of the Human Rights Education Movement of India and is a trustee of the One World Educational Trust. They promote education, empowerment and equal opportunities to Dalits and the rural poor. Most Dalits (untouchables) live in poverty in addition to the social discrimination imposed on them by religion for the past 3000 years. The caste system through religious indoctrination has perpetuated poverty and servitude. Dalit people live in segregated colonies based on discrimination of untouchability and are subject to violent attacks and violation of human rights. We were given a tour of the school that this foundation has built for Dalit students, educating them in nursing and food preparation.

We then were escorted to one of the Dalit villages. I was introduced to Lazar, then one of the community leaders. I met his son, Prabher, and daughter, Lancy. Since our meeting, I have kept all three of them in mind, as was the goal of the toothbrush assignment. My frequent memories spurred me to want to "do something". I had kept in touch with Henry, who helped me with the administrative details of financially helping Prabher and Lancy complete their basic education (equivalent to completion of High School). Lancy had high enough scores that she passed the "12th Standard, equivalent to our Junior College. She now has been accepted into a 4 year Engineering College. I continue to financially support her in that endeavor.

Unfortunately, I have heard that Lazar has been caught in the vicious cycle of unemployment and alcohol. Such is the plight of many in the Dalit villages. Hopefully his children will be able to have an impact on changing this phenomenon in their village.

My financial contributions are minimal compared to what Henry, Lazar, his children, and other Dalits in the village taught me. They taught me that happiness is not related to material possession, that life is not fair but one makes the best of it, and that change can only be brought about by the action of caring individuals coupled with perseverance. My toothbrush person changed my life.

(This photo is of Lazar and my son, Benjamin, who was a student on our Semester at Sea voyage. The picture was not only to remember the face of Lazar but to document his contact information so I would not lose it.)

Chad Nico Hiu, Spring 2004

Lost and Found

When I close my eyes, it is like I am still there; standing beside the one room home, watching as the sun slowly disappears beneath the low hanging clouds surrounding the city. I hear songs echoing in my ears, and feel the weight of a child on my shoulders. A necklace on my desk serves as a tangible reminder of an indescribable connection and friendship.

It was two days before the end of our stay in Salvador, Brazil during the Spring 2004 voyage, and I was searching for something; yet I did not know what that something was. So I left the ship, walked along the coastline, and began a destination-less pilgrimage. For what seemed like hours, I passed neighborhoods and businesses, families picnicking, and children sleeping beneath overpasses. I kept walking.

They say that "When we let go of what we have, we receive what we need." While resting on a rock wall beside a lighthouse, a small voice interrupted my meditation, "Konichiwa!" To my left stood a boy with a contagious smile that spread from ear to ear. He had an energy and spark that seemed to resonate from the core of his spirit. I motioned for him to sit next to me, and in broken Portuguese, we talked about his family, life, music, dreams, and Salvador.

An hour later, Edi and I began walking to our mutual destination. It was lucky I had found him as I had not yet figured out how I was to return to the Pelourinho area, and the S.S. Universe Explorer. Through the rain we continued, aiding and supporting each other, as if we had known each other our whole lives. He asked to go atop my shoulders. I knelt down, and he climbed atop my sun-burned shoulders, securing his hands to my forehead. As we made our way back to Pelourinho, I offered to buy him dinner in exchange for the lessons in Portuguese, and his company. With an air of wisdom well beyond his years, he humbly declined my offer, though he had said that his last meal was breakfast, the day before.

The connection between us deepened with each conversation and shared experience, and he became my companion, guide, and friend. While we walked, he would spontaneously burst out in song and dance in the middle of the street, pulling me along. He seemed so free... undeterred by the challenges he faces on a daily basis. I still hum the songs he sang. We walked by a store, where he disappeared for a second, then reappeared with a necklace, which he tied around my neck. I could not refuse his gift... I didn't have the heart. He now had one real (Brazilian currency) left. The two days we spent together seemed to pass in the blink of an eye.

Three hours before I was to report back on the ship, I was standing atop the side of a hill, about a half hour walk from Pelourinho. Grocery bags in hand, Edi and I were carefully making our way down dirt steps which were stabilized by wooden blocks. As we descended the steep mountain side, I asked Edi where we were going, and he softly replied "home." Turning corner after corner, we finally came upon a proud one room home, with walls of an earthy brown, shielded above by metal paneling of some sort. As we walked through the narrow doorway, he showed me the box of cornflakes I had purchased the day before, and pointed to the little couch that served as his bed. The T.V. that didn't function served as a light source, and he proudly displayed the cupboard where he kept his belongings. Standing besides his home, I asked his father for an address so that I could write them. He said they did not have one, as their home had no house number, so he gave me a tattered, worn piece of paper that resembled a receipt of some sort; still kept in my journal. He told me to show it to someone who could read Portuguese. I told Edi I would do my best, and gave him the biggest hug I could, "Muito quidate," I said into his ear. My eyes glossed over as I walked away.

During the 100 days of the Spring 2004 voyage of Semester at Sea, I was able to visit museums, cultural celebrations and churches, walk along the Atlantic, Indian and Pacific Oceans, eat elegant food, drink under the twilight of dusk, and dance with beautiful women in the pouring rain to the live music of international superstars. Yet when asked about my 'toothbrush' person, now seven years later, one memory sticks with me. I remember lifting Edi onto my shoulders, and the way his smile and laughter seemed to create a feeling of joy so tangible, it was like I could reach out and grab a hold of it. I still hum the songs he sang.

This is a short poem I wrote while sitting on that rock wall beside the light house, just before Edi found me... having now traveled to 25 countries across the globe and dedicating my life to enabling others to experience all the world has to offer, it became my life's mission statement:

To see what I have not seen
To learn what I do not know
To go where I have not gone
To walk freely and unfettered
To live with opened eyes
To love from the depths of my soul

Jennie Karalewich, Spring 2004

My toothbrush person story is a bit different from other toothbrush stories out there. In my story, I didn't make eye contact with someone on a street, I wasn't invited on an impromptu tour by a mysterious stranger, or witnessed something shocking. My experience was arranged, a bit more planned if you will, however it was as memorable, spontaneous, or soul stirring as any other story you'll read.

The minute I was accepted to Semester at Sea Spring 2004, I sang the memorized itinerary in my head and I could feel the breeze across my face in Cape Town while standing between the Atlantic and Table Mountain or could see myself walking through crowded market stalls in Vietnam. This pattern repeated for most of the countries on the itinerary. However I was drawing a blank for India, how can you prepare for India? Between the size of the country and all of the sites to see, I was intimidated and stuck.

A dear friend of mine at Penn State, Raya, was born in India and grew up in Nigeria. I began to bug Raya about what to do during my stay in India. I am not sure who originally suggested meeting his family in Chennai but the idea stuck and plans were made.

The moment I met Raya's Aunt Saranya in Chennai I felt like I was a member of her family, a missing niece. There was no forced formality when we met, there was an instant connection.

The next two days I was made a member of the family. I got to meet several of Saranya's sisters: Sathya, Varala, Padma, Paddu, and Saraswathi (Paddu's sister-in-law). Meals incorporated corn on the cob and pumpkin (and less spicy) because I was an American and they would be familiar tastes for me after being away for two months. I got to eat from a bowl of pomegranate seeds that would magically refill despite the labor intensive peeling process. In the evening, Saranya's niece took me to see a Bollywood movie drive in style.

I feel its important to note that I am not writing this to impress others with my experience or list everything I did travelogue style. I just want to convey that Saranya and her extended family embraced me as a family member despite not knowing me. After being at sea for two months and seeing a lot of things spanning from amazing to thrilling to shocking to disturbing in a short span of time, it was a time I needed to be embraced.

Now that you read my story, I feel that I should note that Saranya was 82 years old at the time and her family ranged in age from 83-74 and Vidya was 35.

I hope all is going well.
Keep brushing your teeth!

dag1@psu.edu

Veronica Regueiro, Spring 2004
2004

My toothbrush image is not just one person. One person cannot sum up all of India; one image cannot hold India. My toothbrush image is India as a whole. India broke my heart. Yes, the poverty and destitution and lack of clean water are horrible - but there is a spiritual starvation and a hopelessness there that stuck to my skin and filled my pores. I can't condense or process all of it, because to do so would be to cut away some part, to peel away something that is vital and thus destroy the canvas that is India. Well . . . maybe it all can be contained in one image: a naked little boy, an orange string tied around his waist, his hair hanging in his face, lifting his arms and straining towards my bus window from the dirty, crowd-infested sidewalk. He must have been two, and he was filthy. But he was smiling at me and I realized that his entire life, his smile had been his way to survive. That little hand reaching up towards me will be with me forever, even as the words "don't give to the beggars" beat out their rhythm in my head.

Semester at Sea changes you in a way that is unexpected. Of course, you get on the ship and you expect to have adventures and you expect to learn. You know that you're going to see things that most of your fellow Americans will never see. The part that caught me by surprise was how once you see something, you can't un-see it.

India was an . . . interesting . . . place for me as a twenty year old college student sailing around the world. They tell you on the ship that you will never be further from home, in terms of distance or in terms of culture, and I think that it's fair to say that that is a massive understatement. Being in India was the first time that I had seen a city where literally everyone lives on the street, where people die of starvation while cows saunter by, where mothers maim their children to make them better beggars because their place in society dictates that a beggar is all they will ever be.

For a while after my trip, I wanted to forget India, but as I have gotten older, as I and the world have changed, India has come to mean new things for me. India is a reminder to be grateful for living in a land where I have opportunities to advance myself. It's a reminder to be thankful for food and clean water. India reminds me that most of the world doesn't live the way I live, that there are billions of people on this planet who go to bed hungry or thirsty or curled up in the rain because they don't have a roof over their heads. These are things I think about whenever I brush my teeth. It sounds odd, but I have always kept the essay I wrote in Global Studies in my medicine cabinet. Whenever I open the cabinet, I see the folded square of paper on which I originally wrote the words above and I see the note from Don printed on the outside and I remember how lucky I am and that there are people out there with far less than me. It seemed like a silly assignment at the time but that little piece of paper, waiting to greet me in the morning and then again at the end of the day, reminds me to be compassionate, to conserve resources, to be thankful. I am reminded of this whenever I open the medicine cabinet, whenever I brush my teeth.

Funny how important a toothbrush can be.

Jennifer Utz, Spring 2004

I wasn't a student on the voyage, but rather a staff member. I was the video editor who compiled hours of incredible footage into a feature documentary about the students' journey around the world. Digging through the 80 hours of footage and crafting a narrative wasn't easy, I must say. But it was powerful. From my home editing studio in Portland, Oregon, I viewed endless hours of footage of young students seeing the world - the REAL world - for the first time. I frequently teared up as I watched the footage. They were breaking out of the shell from which they had been exposed to their whole lives. It was beautiful.

My toothbrush person is a woman who was selling produce at a market in Pondicherry, India. I asked to take her picture and she obliged. She insisted upon putting a row of jasmine in my hair and we took a photo together. I continued to photograph more produce vendors in the market, who were all incredibly kind and welcoming to someone who was clearly an outsider.

When I returned to the States, I sent prints of the photos I had taken at the market to a vendor who had given me his address.

I returned to live in India in 2005 to teach filmmaking to members of ANANDI (a women's empowerment organization). I went back to Pondicherry, visited the market and the vendor to whom I had sent the photos. He poured me a cup of chai and we spoke in broken English about our lives. Then he showed me that he had framed the photos I'd mailed him, as well as the letter I had sent with them. I was delighted that they'd remembered me and that they had appreciated the small gift I had given them, which was not nearly as much as they had given me.

Adrienne Volk, Spring 2004

It was a warm, sunny day in Cape Town, South Africa just over a month into my Semester at Sea Spring 2004 voyage. I was participating in a tour of one of the largest townships in the country with the Amy Biehl Foundation. My senses were overwhelmed with sights, sounds and smells that were foreign to me. One sight, in particular, struck me as I turned a corner walking down the dusty road. A beautiful little girl, with dark chocolate skin and a bright pink sun dress, sat perched on a pile of garbage bags. She wasn't in school or daycare, like a child should be on a Monday afternoon, and she just sat and stared, not saying a word. This little girl touched me instantly. Luckily, I had sunglasses on which hid the tears that welled in my eyes. I couldn't help but wonder where she came from, where her parents were and why she was sitting on that pile of garbage and not at school. The irony of the beautiful girl sitting on that pile of garbage sent shivers down my spine. I took a picture to remember her and remember the lessons that she unknowingly taught me. I have had that picture inside of my bathroom vanity since 2004 so that each time I brush my teeth, I am reminded of her lessons. I am reminded that I am so fortunate for all of the blessings in my life: that I was always loved, provided for and taken care of as a child, that I was educated in wonderful schools, that I was born in a country where I have rights as a woman and that I have so many luxuries such as a warm and safe home with running water and a toilet that flushes. It's these blessings that I often take for granted, but when faced with the reality of most of the world, that I am reminded of just how fortunate I truly am.

1990 Toothbrush Memories

There are not many student reflections in this section of the book. I think there are four major reasons for this limited response from 1990 students.

First it was a smaller group of students than in 2004, and 2010. I think the cohort from 1990 was approximately 520. In 2004, the number of students increased to 600; and in 2010 there were approximately 675 students on board. So the numbers were larger in the later years.

Secondly, this was the first time that I had tried the toothbrush assignment and I think I just had them think over and make mental notes about their toothbrush people. I did not have them write a "letter", only close their eyes and think about a person they had met. Obviously there were no letters to mail back to them. So over time, there was more zeal by me about this project. The 1990 students were the first time that I tried this exercise.

Thirdly, the technology has dramatically changed since 1990. Now, most voyages have a face book page to stay in contact. They also stay up with their email and it is easier to contact recent students. And to have the picture of the "toothbrush person" necessitates a look in the dusty album in the desk for most – no digital photos in those days.

Finally, not everyone will remember a college memory from 21 years ago when brushing your teeth.

Having said all of this, I hope you enjoy these memories from over twenty-two years ago.

1990
Photographs &
Comments

Glenn Broadley, Fall 1990

When I sailed on the F90 voyage, I lived in a very small town on Cape Cod called Cataumet. I was the true fish out of water as I left my small sea side town to embark on the around the world voyage. Never before I left had the world seemed like such a big place. I was very overwhelmed as the voyage began. This was intensified by spraining my ankle the third day out. Now, in addition to being overwhelmed, I was down right discouraged. I have never told any one until now, but at that time, I seriously considered going home once we reached Japan. When we got to Japan, I met my tooth brush person. His name was Geairo and he attended the Kansi University in Kobe Japan. I participated in an inport adventure where members of the English department from Kansi, hosted SAS students for a day. They showed us around Kobe and Osaka. We got to see Japan, they got to use their English. It was a win win. With my ankle still in a lot of pain, and harboring my clandestine anxiety about this voyage I gave the day my all. I asked a lot of questions and enjoyed the company of Geairo and his classmates. At one point I asked if any of them had been to the United States. Geairo said he had and that he was an exchange student for a month. He talked of staying on Cape Cod. I of course perked up and asked where he had stayed. Geairo suggested that even coming from Cape Cod I probably had not heard of the place he stayed where it was such a small town. Imagine my shock when Geairo uttered the word Cataumet??? My mouth literally dropped. Not only had he stayed in my town, but on my same road!!! Suddenly, the world did not seem so big and the trip not so overwhelming. I was told that after Japan, everyone on the voyage would change a bit and that was a true statement. I realized how petty I was being, found new enthusiasm and gave that voyage everything I had. I have never forgotten Geairo and every day of my life since the voyage, I have reflected on some part of it.

Scott Downs & Kristen Johnson, Fall 1990

Boy meets girl; weds decade later.

Two college students from the North East met on the ship somewhere near Japan. Our first date was in Keelung Taiwan to the Yehliu "Geo" National seashore. I played basketball with Taiwanese children at hoops near the park while she watched, we explored the unique coastline and navigated the city by bus with a map together. She knew I wanted to kiss her, but that would have to wait………

We travelled a bit in different ports, like young adults on again / off again when our paths crossed. Since we were travelling around the world, our paths crossed in each country we visited. As like a whirlwind, we danced together in Ned Kelly's in Hong Kong, hiked the seven wells slides then dipped in the ocean under the stars on the Malaysian island of Langkawi.

From the confines of the ship to the wide open plains, we Safari'ed in Kenya in the shadow of Mt. Kilimanjaro and experienced the hustle & bustle of Mombasa on a dirt motorcycle I rented to get around the city.

We sunbathed on the ship's "steel beach" with our friends and once in Salvador Bahia (Brazil) we tried to Lambada in their large dance halls. Winding long into the morning, we'd usually end of under the stars listening to the ocean crash on the rocks under our hotel balcony.

When we returned to Port Everglades, she only had a few hours before her return flight home, so I took her to the airport, and with our voyage, started a relationship which, after the ship, has been 22 years in duration. While this book is about our Tooth Brush person, I can't say I think about her every time I brush my teeth, but I can say she is the most influential person I met on Semester at Sea and I can say I park my toothbrush next to hers in the medicine cabinet every night and into the unforeseeable future.

Don Gogniat, Fall 1990

In 1990 on a trip to Japan I thought it would be a cultural experience to go to a Japanese hot spring for a traditional Japanese hot tub type soak. Near Kobe, up the mountain on a tram, is a local resort called Arima Hot Springs. It sounded perfect; I took the tram up the mountain overlooking Kobe to a Swiss-like setting. I did not know the rules of the place, but it seemed that you bought a ticket, checked your clothes and then entered segregated pools of water that got progressively hotter. I like the heat so this part of the experience was fine. It appeared that I was the only non Japanese in the place. It also appeared that I was the youngest person in the place (45 at the time). These were all old Japanese men. All of these people had probably fought in World War II. Certainly all had memories of the war. All of these men probably had some experience with American troops either before or after the surrender. And all of them had lived through the atomic bombs of Hiroshima and Nagasaki. Here we were in a pool of hot water, only our heads bobbing around looking at each other and knowing that we were from such different places and with such different experiences. It is hard not to stretch your imagination and wonder what thoughts must have been going through their minds. My nonexistent Japanese certainly didn't help to break the silence. Only slight smiles and an appreciation for the warmth of the water (as signaled nonverbally) was all that we uttered to each other.

What were they thinking about this 45 year old American in their hot spring? Did they forgive the second atomic bomb? Did they feel comfortable with the globalized world that had developed after the war? Did they appreciate that most of Hawaii was now being bought with Japanese money from surplus trade? Were they like every other generation wondering what happened to the young and why they were so different from when they were young?

I left the Springs feeling reflective, and somber. Tomorrow I would take the train to Hiroshima and I knew the faces in the water would stay with me.

Occasionally, today when I brush my teeth, I still think about those men - and lately this leads to thoughts of nuclear weapons, and old men in Iraq, and Iran and Afghanistan.

Briavel Holcomb, Fall 1990

I sailed first on SAS in Fall 1990. I was teaching on the ship and my daughter, Genevieve, was a student. Crossing the Pacific, I talked in my classes about the geography and cities of Japan. Then we docked and spent several days exploring the environs of Kobe. When we resumed classes as we sailed towards Taiwan, my students said, in effect, that Japan wasn't what they had expected – that my descriptions had not adequately prepared them. Indeed, I had never been to Japan before so all I knew about it was learned from books (no Web in those days!). But that reinforced for me the huge advantage of experiential learning. There is no substitute for actually being in a place. The first evening in Kobe I went into town with Sally Alexander, who is blind. I was fascinated to understand how she received audio, touch, smell and kinetic clues from the environment and constructed her detailed understanding of our surroundings, while my impressions were mostly visual images. Nevertheless, discussing our walk later, we had overlapping place memories.

One of my resolutions before starting our voyage was that I would spend at least half a day in each port exploring by myself. While there are, of course, lots of advantages of one or more traveling companions who can help with wayfinding, keep track of things, share experiences and expenses, and generally ameliorate loneliness, companions also insulate you from the experience. So on one of the first days in Kobe, I walked to the top of the hills overlooking the port. Several people greeted me en route, and I replied in English/non verbally. At the summit there was an engraved map/scenic view which labeled (in Japanese) various features. A man was nearby and although he spoke no English, and I spoke no Japanese, he pointed to features on the map and then on the landscape explaining the landscape before us. He then communicated that there was a scenic route back down the hill and he and I walked back down to Kobe together.

This Fall (2011) I went back to Kobe with SAS. This time I went on a field trip to see some of the consequences of the 1995 earthquake including a museum where part of the fault line is preserved, and an institute where mitigation measures and research is carried out. I did not see my toothbrush person again, but I hope he survived the earthquake. He and Sally (with whom I am still in touch) both taught me valuable lessons about ways of perceiving and communicating environmental messages.

Megan Winterhalter-Lizewski, Fall 1990

I recall being nervous about going into China. Before leaving Pittsburgh, PA, my dad had gently warned me to exercise caution during my travels – especially in China, and he then whispered, "Remember what we watched of Tiananmen Square." His serious tone was still discernible as I sailed from Hong Kong to mainland China, and I reminded myself of the need to be mindful of what I said and did.

We arrived at Guangzhou University in the Guangdong province after several hours of traveling. After a restless night, I was introduced to Jane, a Chinese student ambassador. Though much of my Semester at Sea journey of twenty-some years ago is a blur, my time with Jane is quite clear. She was studying English at the university, and she was thrilled that I was an English Literature major. Within minutes of meeting her, my fears of being in China dissolved. We spent the first hour talking about Jane Austin, a writer we both admired.

Her awe of my video camera and my surprise upon seeing her stark dormitory room were clear reminders of the many differences that existed between the two of us, yet as we traveled from one site to the next, we huddled together in our bus seat whispering and giggling like two young school girls.

I met dozens of memorable and remarkable people that fall of 1990, and many left impressions on me, but my encounter with Jane is the one that continues to remind me that though mountains, deserts, oceans, languages, and cultures may separate us, we share the common thread of humanity.

Lynn Sayre Visser, Fall 1990

A Face without a Name

As the years have passed, my toothbrush person has evolved into a collection of faces, but one face continually comes to the forefront of my thoughts. When I envision my time on Semester at Sea, a flash flood of memories engulfs every synapse in my brain. Several snapshots of memories are frozen in time, yet detailed as if the experience was yesterday. Boarding the ship in Canada, I didn't know a single person. My emotions ran from excitement to fear. As a twenty-year old college student, I was preparing to leave United States soil for the very first time. Zero contact with family would occur until I reached Japan 14 days later. For the next 108 days most of my communication would occur through letters and a rare phone call. The adventures that were in store for me on the voyage ahead would transform me as a person, solidify my values, determine my ultimate career path, and shape me into the healthcare professional I am today. Seeing the world first hand was the gift of a lifetime, forever treasured, and never taken for granted.

As the ship approached India, the shipboard faculty repeatedly told the students "don't give to the beggars". Concern lingered regarding our safety; if we gave to one beggar, we could potentially be swarmed by others. Pick pocketing in India was a real concern. For three days I ignored the beggars; trying not to make eye contact with the people I was tremendously curious about seemed to lessen my pain. Walking away from a man with only one arm and one leg left me feeling physically nauseated. Traveling the country by taxi and bus brought countless experiences of children chasing the vehicle, arms outstretched, pleading for something to be given to them. Anything tangible would have been more than what most of these children had.

Internal conflict ensued as I struggled to follow the directions of the shipboard faculty. My heart was telling me to give to the beggars. On day four, I couldn't take it anymore. Stuck in traffic in New Dehli, a young girl reached through the partially rolled down taxi window. She repeatedly touched my arm and then outstretched her hand all while moaning simultaneously. That moment is forever etched in my brain. The pain on her face instantly stripped my heart to the core. I wondered why she appeared to be in such agony. Was she hungry? Did she have family? Where did she sleep at night? Why was she all alone? With only a limited number of rupees in my wallet, I pulled out a ten dollar bill from the thin wallet that I hid underneath my skirt. I placed the money into her hand. Tears filled my eyes as I rolled up the window and the taxi drove away. The name of my toothbrush person will never be known, but the imprint she made on my mind, heart, and soul will continue to touch me forever.

Chapter Four

You Too Can Have a Toothbrush Person

You don't have to travel around the world to have a toothbrush person. It is just a matter of appreciating the moment, and then taking advantage of some stimulus to remember this good time. Here are two stories that will serve as examples. The first story is the genesis for "inventing" toothbrush people.

Walking Past a Bakery in the Southside of Pittsburgh

"Take time to smell the roses" is one of ten travel tips that I give to students having an international experience. The key word here, however, is "smell". I remember walking down Carson St. in the South Side ethnic neighborhood of Pittsburgh Pennsylvania. As I walked by a bakery the smell of freshly baked rye bread blasted out the front door. A few moments later a felt twinge of melancholy and had no idea how this change of mood took place. It took a couple of days of thinking about this event to finally understand what had happened on that fall day. I remember the smell of rye bread baking when I first learned that my grandmother had died. The rye smell and her death must have been hardwired into my brain. Now when I smell rye bread I know that thoughts of my grandmother may pop into my head. Now the smell doesn't linger around melancholy, but moves on to nice memories of the times I'd spent with that old caring women who came from the Ukraine.

I learned a lot from that moment in the South Side and I think it really has changed my life. I'm sure most of you already know most of this, but for me here is the lesson from rye bread:

> *When you are happy and feeling very good about something - savor the moment. Take time to fill your senses with everything that is around you. Look at the color of the sky. Smell the things near you. Touch something. Really appreciate this happy moment with all of your senses. Someday you may be walking on your own "South Side" and a twinge of happiness comes over you. You may not have any idea why this has happened, but it just may be because that smell or maybe that blue sky is the exact same color you filed away when you took time to appreciate that happy moment in the past. Your subconscious brain remembers that color and that you were happy when you saw it.*

It seems to "make sense" to take time and appreciate a great moment for what it is. It will come back to you in ways you can't imagine. So the travel tip of "take time to smell the roses" is a little more complicated than that, but it is a great start for sure. Really take time to smell, touch, feel, and see the roses. Taste doesn't work here, but you get what I mean.

The second story also is another travel tip; and that is:

Listen with your ears <u>and your heart</u>.

It is very very hard to be a good listener if you are an American. It is possible, but it takes practice and the full faith that something worthwhile will come from listening. I learned this from my mother. She hand-stitched a Pennsylvania Dutch saying and put it in a frame and gave it to me. It says "you ain't learnin' when you're talkin'". I found this to be good advice and kept it with me throughout my life – usually above my desk and near the phone. Listening with an open mind and an open heart (empathy) is the synonym for compassion. This may be hard to do, but worth the effort.

"Toothbrush people" are really just disciplined moments of good thoughts, and good interactions where everyone is really listening and appreciating each other. The moment is captured through emotions and senses and then consciously programmed to be recalled with a certain stimulus (in this case, brushing your teeth).

We invite you to practice "toothbrush people behavior" and see what happens. You know songs bring you back to events and people from the past. Sometimes they are good memories and sometimes not so good. The point of this book is to make sure that good experiences aren't wasted for the future. In the moment, file away good experiences through all kinds of senses (to take advantage of your unconscious) and then consciously decide to think back to them when brushing your teeth, or any activity that you think would be a good trigger for remembering good thoughts. I like "toothbrush" because it starts your day off with a good feeling. It is your choice, but give it a try and see if it makes you happier.

Good luck and put the cap back on.

Postscript

As you may remember from one of the letters of students from 1990, Scott Downs and Kristen Johnson talk about meeting on the ship and later getting married. This is a rare event, but certainly not the only time that it has happened in the long history of Semester at Sea.

Todd Miller also met Joselyn Pomeroy on their 1984 voyage and married a year later. They have stayed involved with Semester at Sea, and in fact Todd is presently on the Board of Directors. I mention them here not for the marital bliss that these couples seem to enjoy, but because of an interesting non-profit organization that Todd and Joselyn have founded. "Global Grins" gives free toothbrushes to people who need them throughout the world – hundreds of thousands of toothbrushes have been distributed to over 80 countries. It just seems appropriate for a book called "Toothbrush People", based on stories from Semester at Sea, to try and make others aware of this important program. To understand exactly what they are doing go to:

www.globalgrins.org

Todd and Joselyn need our support, and the program is another example of small changes that make a big difference. Congratulations.

About the Authors

Don Gogniat worked as an administrator for Penn State University from 1986 - 2005. He was the Campus Executive Officer at Penn State York from 1993- 2003; and from 2003 – 2005, he was the Director of International Programs for the Commonwealth College of Penn State. Additionally since 1993, he has been teaching geography courses each year for Penn State.

His PhD is in Cultural Geography from the University of Pittsburgh (1983); he received an M.A. in Geography from Indiana University of Pa. (1973), and a B.S. in Education from Indiana University of Pa. (1970). He joined the Peace Corps (Costa Rica, 1974-75) and worked as a regional planner for the Costa Rican National Planning Office. Gogniat has sailed on Semester at Sea where he taught geography in the fall of 1985, and Global Studies in fall of 1990 and spring of 2004, and spring of 2010. He was the Executive Dean on the summer voyage in 2006. He taught a course for teachers on the summer 2008 voyage entitled "Globalizing the Curriculum". He is scheduled to teach Global Studies again in the fall of 2012.

His hobbies are travel, billiards and photography. His photographic work has appeared in newspapers, magazines, and juried exhibits. He also believes that your age should never get larger than the number of countries you have explored.

Valerie D. White is an academic reference librarian living in York, PA. She has previously worked at Penn State York and Tarrant County College in Fort Worth, TX.

Her MLS is from Texas Woman's University (2000), she has a B.A. in Political Science from Moravian College (1986), and is certified as a Montessori instructor.

She is married with one daughter and a dog. Favorite pastimes include puzzles, reading (a librarian who reads!), and travel.